# THE ART OF STRETCHING AND KICKING

by James Lew

I&I SPORTS
MARTIAL ARTS SUPPLIES & ACCESSORIES

# Acknowledgements

I would like to give my special thanks for all the help, encouragement and advice offered by my martial arts colleagues and warm personal friends, Albert Leong and Sifu Douglas Wong.

James Lew

# About the Author

Over the past eleven years, kung-fu has been more than a way of life for James Lew. He's used it as a vehicle to launch a sucessful tournament career winning consecutive grand championship at every major West Coast kung-fu, karate tournament.

He's used the arts as a springboard to a sucessful business career an an instructor and school owner in Los Angeles, California.

His affiliation with the arts has landed any number of parts in several motion pictures including "The Killing of a Chinese Bookie" produced by John Cassavetes, a host of television parts including credits on the series "Kung-Fu," and was a cast member in a major Las Vegas production dealing with the martial arts. James is continuing his acting career with a number of upcoming projects in both films and television.

But the publication business is nothing new to the young sifu either. For more than four years he has served as an active technical advisor and publication assistant with *Inside Kung-Fu* magazine.

In addition, the energetic kung-fu stylist utilized his academic background as a business major to take over the complicated aspects of merchandising and marketing for Mantis Supply Company.

A lifelong athlete and physical culture enthusiast, James has always been interested in bodybuilding and nutrition. While a student, he participated in gymnastics, skiing, horseback riding, tennis and ballet.

The stretching exercises put forth in this book are a result of years of athletic training and study which have helped him to maximize his performance in every sport endeavor he has undertaken. Their worth has been substantiated by hundreds of his grateful students.

The excitement he has already generated with this, his first book, has prompted him to begin on still another dealing with bodybuilding and its application to the martial arts.

# Foreword

As anyone familiar with Kung-Fu knows, kicking techniques vary from style to style. Northern forms of Kung-Fu have been noted for strenuous, energetic leg maneuvers while southern styles have traditionally leaned toward kicks of a more conservative nature. The old Chinese saying, "Nan-Chuan, Pei-Tui" (Hands in the south, kicks in the north) refers to this division.

Some historians maintain that the reason for the north's preference of leg maneuvers over hand techniques can be boiled down to the northern terrain and climate. The northern countryside has large expanses of plains. Its climate is harsh, but there is room to move. In the more densely populated south, with its tropical climate, Kung-Fu practitioners were forced to confine their practice to smaller areas–more often than not, boats or barges, requiring solid stances for maintaining balance and stability.

Much of the Kung-Fu of the south was perpetuated by actors and operatic stars whose roles required proficiency in the martial arts. Stage actors were divided into three main categories: those who could act; those who specialized in Kung-Fu techniques; and those who could both act and perform the intricate Kung-Fu maneuvers. These actors, most of whom traveled by boat, depicted stories of war heroes of China's turbulent past and were responsible for perpetuating much of what we know to be Kung-Fu.

The north's preference for kicks, others say, can be attributed to regional adherence to religious ideals which also influenced the art of Kung-Fu. Northern Chinese religious tendencies leaned toward Buddhist teachings which, as legends have it, were shaped by the patriarch of Chan Buddhism. They centered around external, muscular training designed to remedy the Shaolin monks deteriorating condition (caused by remaining in static meditative postures). In the south, however, religious tendencies leaned toward the Taoist philosophies. There was formed a distinct division between the northern, physically oriented Kung-Fu (and kicking techniques) and the southern, intellectually oriented training. Active, strenuous exercise was incompatible with the philosophical principles of the Taoist tenets in many ways.

Still other historians, such as William C.C. Hu (ranking among the most respected Kung-Fu historians writing in the English language today) suggest the whole "Nan-Chuan, Pei-Tui" idea may be nothing more than "an oft-repeated melodic ditty" maintained by popular but unsubstantiated beliefs, somehow entwined with another popular saying, "Nan-Ch'uan Pei-Ma," which refers to the *boats* in the south and *horses* in the north. And there is an impressive array of material to back up Hu's suggestion, for many southern stylists were well known for their kicks. Mok-Cheng-Chia, for instance, founded one of the basic systems of southern boxing (Mok-Gar) primarily on the kicking techniques for which he was famous. Wong-Fei-Hong of the Hung-Fa school (immortalized by Kwan-Tak-Hing in his movie-screen portrayals) was famous for his *no-shadow* kick, reputedly so fast it was invisible. By the same token, many northern stylists became famous for their exemplary hand maneuvers. On the whole, however, I am of the opinion that the old saying about kicks in the north holds true, for it refers to the *type* of kicking taught and the *way* in which the kicks were intended to be used. It was not intended to mean that there were no kicks in the south or no hands in the north.

Kicks of southern stylists reflect a conservative attitude toward their use. Kicks are directed, for the most part, to the lower-gate (legs, knees, groin, etc.), while kicks of the north, decidedly more energetic in nature, are more often than not aimed at the mid and upper-gate of the body. Southern stylists don't usually perform the complex jump-kicks or flamboyant spinning wheel-kicks seen in northern systems. The techniques of formal karate suggest its northern Kung-Fu origin. The high, kicking maneuvers of Tae-Kwon-Do also point to such a beginning for although Tae-Kwon Do is a fairly modern art-form (developed and christened by Choi-Hong-Hai) it is based on much older martial systems (Kwan-Pup, Tang-Soo-Do, etc.), which are of essentially northern Kung-Fu origin. Okinawan Karate, too, has long been understood to have been a direct descendant of northern Kung-Fu, the characters for *Kara* and *Te* originally meaning "ohina-hand" until being changed by the Japanese after the arts inception to that country to mean "empty-hand."

Regardless of where kicking originated, which style has the most, or highest, or best, one thing is certain: Using one's feet as well as one's hands is an essential part of Eastern martial systems. If you're going to learn Kung-Fu, Karate or Tae-Kwon-Do, you're going to have to learn about them. And if you're going to have to learn about them, this book will be an asset.

# CONTENTS

# PART ONE

## c] Strhir.ercises

ere Thgreat many stretching exercises, all of which have value. Stretching is without a doubt one of the most beneficial, general exercises one can do. It loosens the tightened, knotted, tensed muscles and tendons which inhibit circulation and relaxation.

The stretching exercises shown here are specialized. They're meant to improve one's kicking ability, kicking height and speed. It cannot be overemphasized, however, that these exercises should be practiced slowly—with caution. Relax into the positions shown. Don't force them. Adjust naturally. Keys to success are relaxation and perseverance. Exercise daily, without fail, and you will begin to feel a new surge of energy freely circulating through your body.

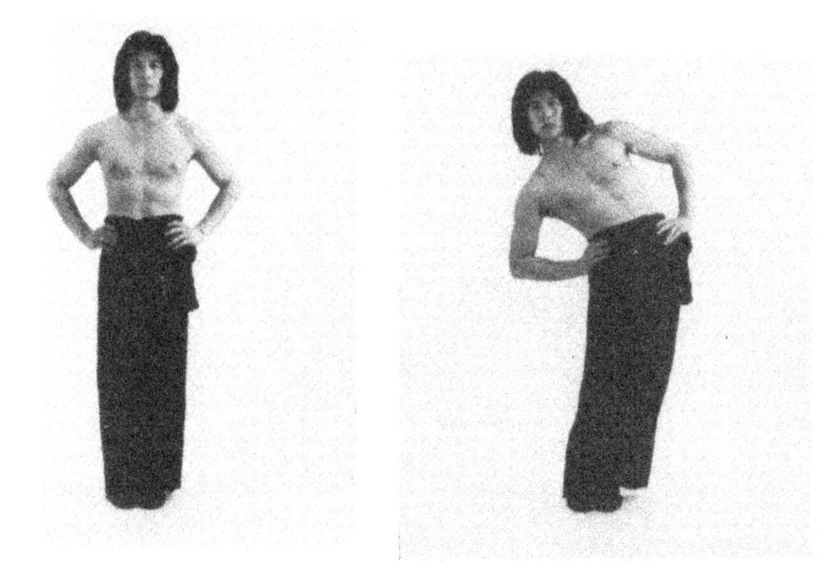

## Hip-Swivel

Stand straight up with your feet together, hands on hips. Keeping your legs straight, lean as far to your left as you can. Swivel your upper torso around clockwise, stretching the muscles in your back, abdomen and sides.

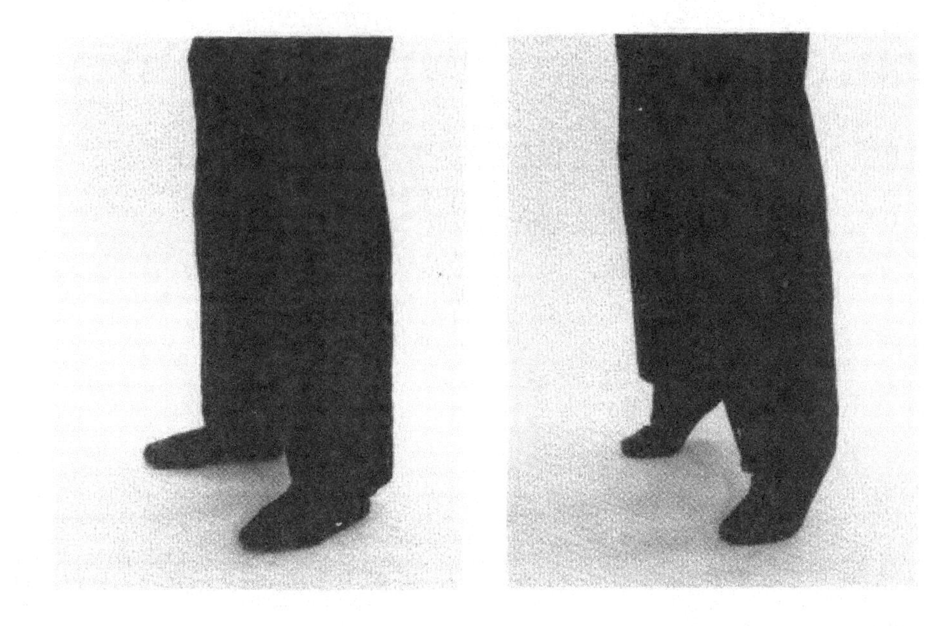

## Ankle Stretch

From a standing position raise up as far as you can on your toes. Dropping your heels back to the floor twist in on your ankles as shown. Twist your feet back to a normal standing position and pull up on your toes.

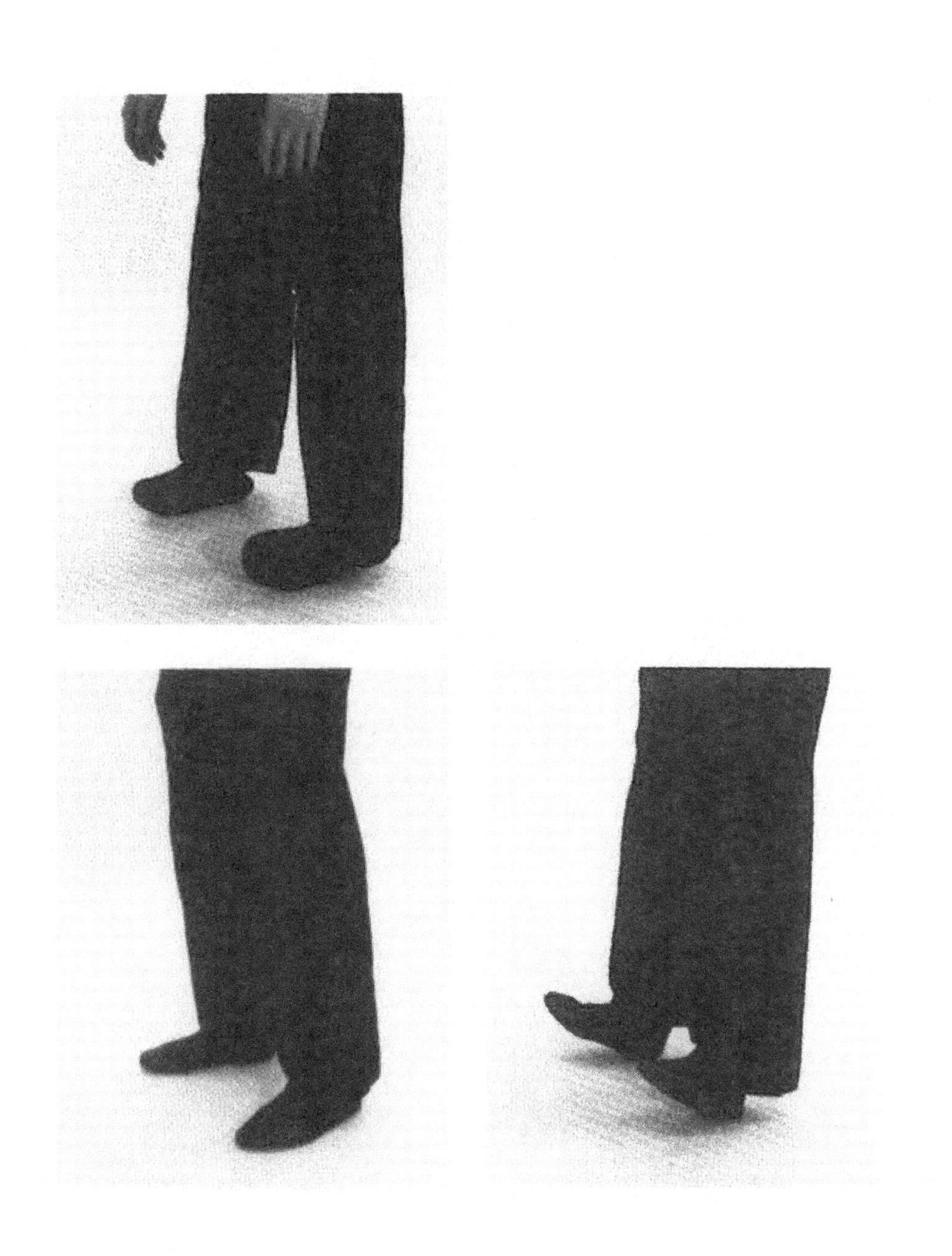

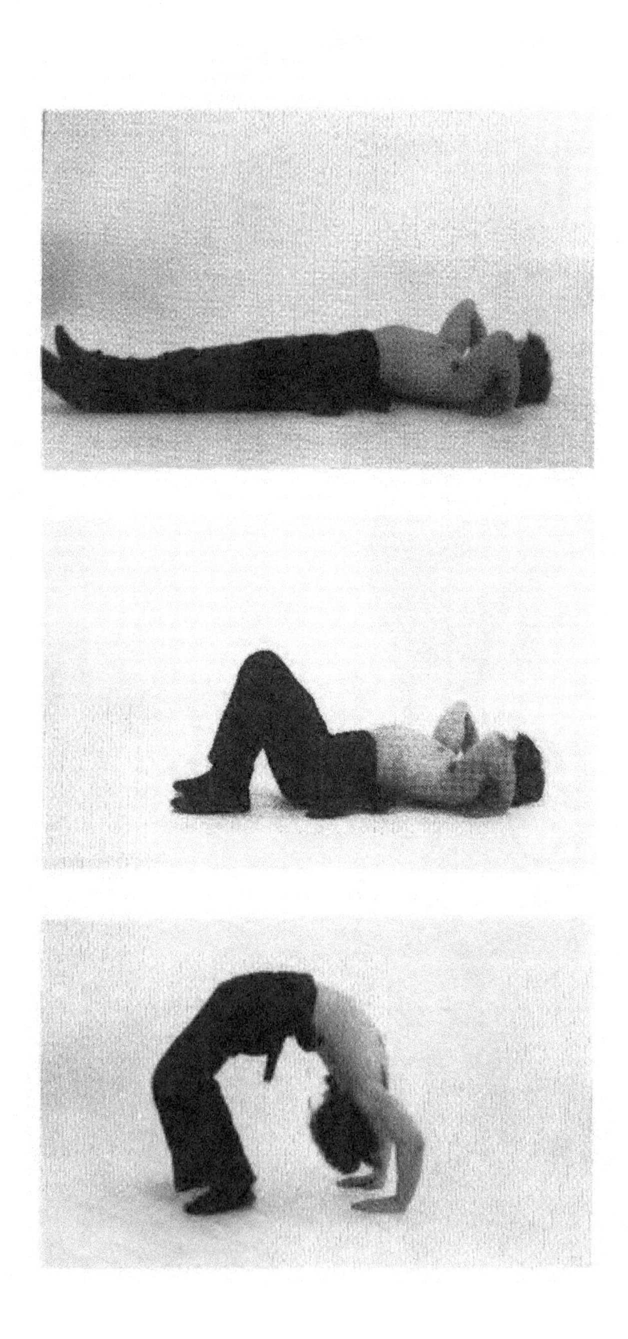

**Back-Arch**

Lie flat on the floor. Draw your heels up next to your buttocks as shown and arch up, pushing with your feet and hands.

**Leg-Twist**

Place your weight onto your right leg and touch the floor with your hands as illustrated. Twist your right leg under your body and lower yourself onto it.

**Single-Splits**

Squatting down on your left leg, extend your right leg out as shown. Bending at the waist, lean as far to the right as possible, then reverse the direction. Complete the exercise by turning back to the right, grasping the extended foot to pull your body all the way down until your forehead touches your knee.

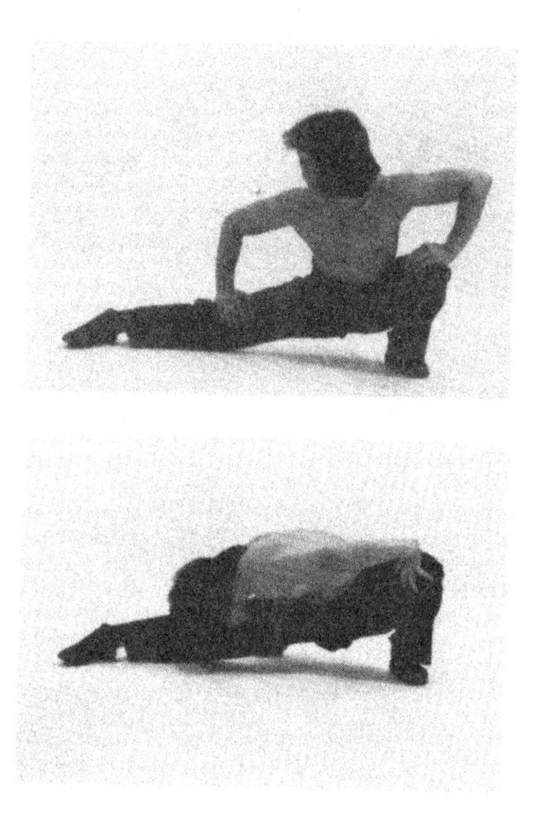

## Forward-Bending Stretch

Keep both legs straight with your feet together. Bend over and touch your fingertips to the ground. Slowly advance by touching your knuckles, then wrists, then palms to the ground until you are able to bring your head between your knees as shown.

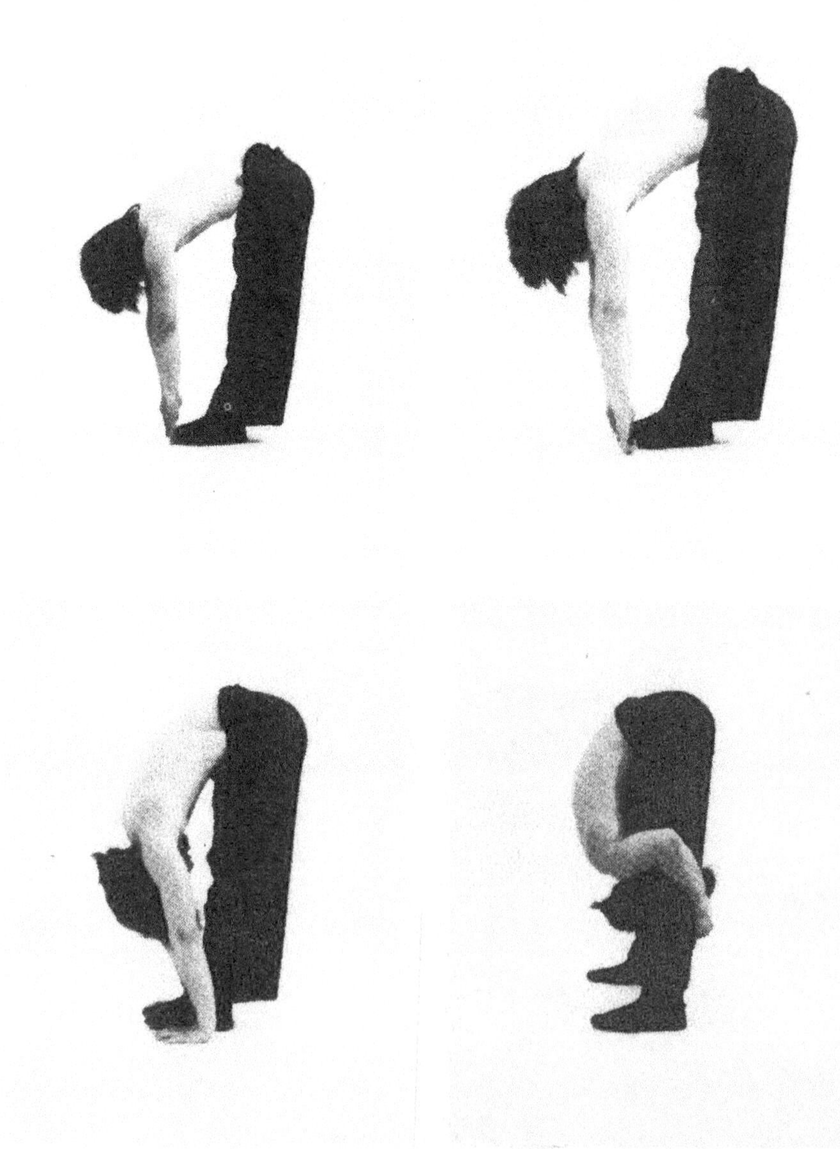

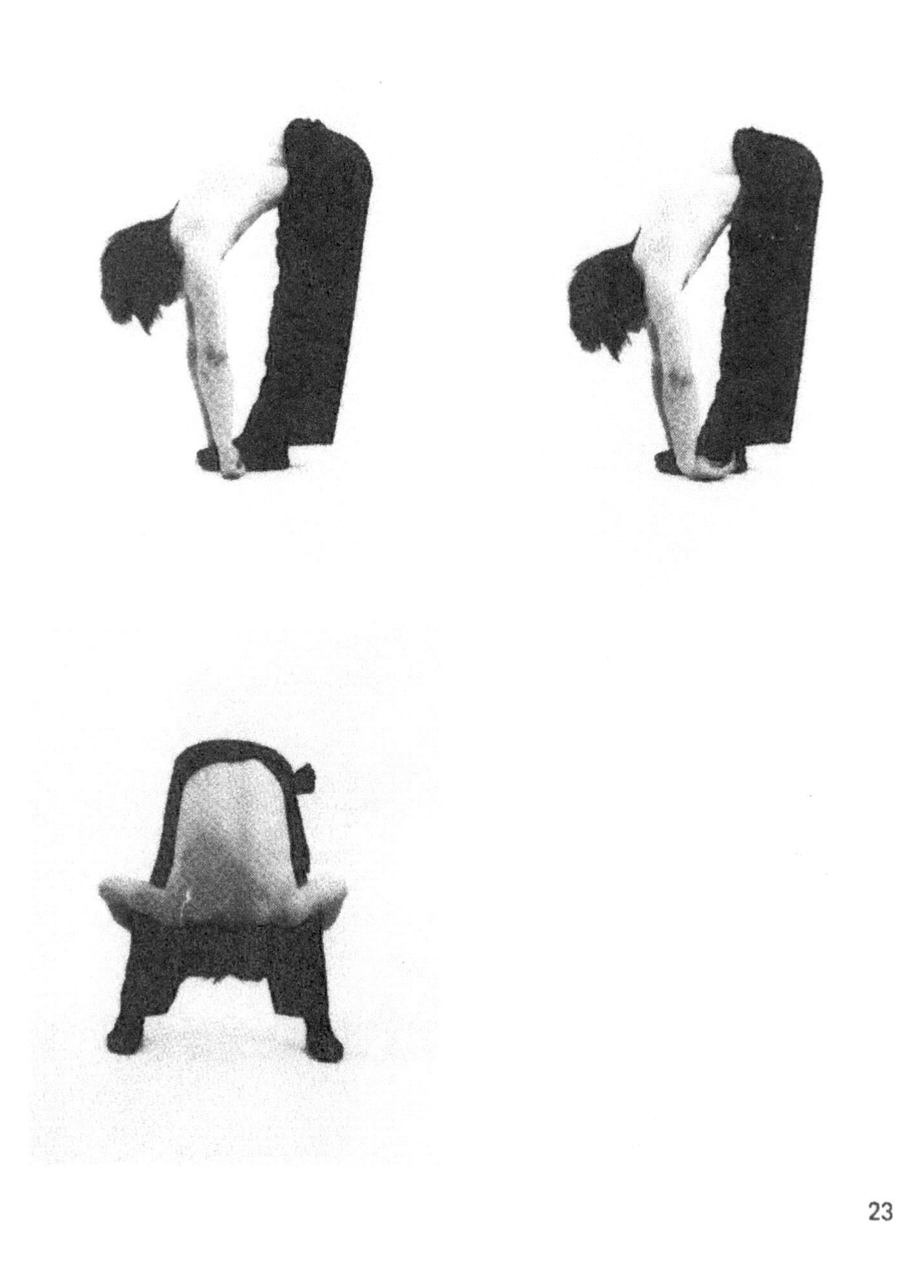

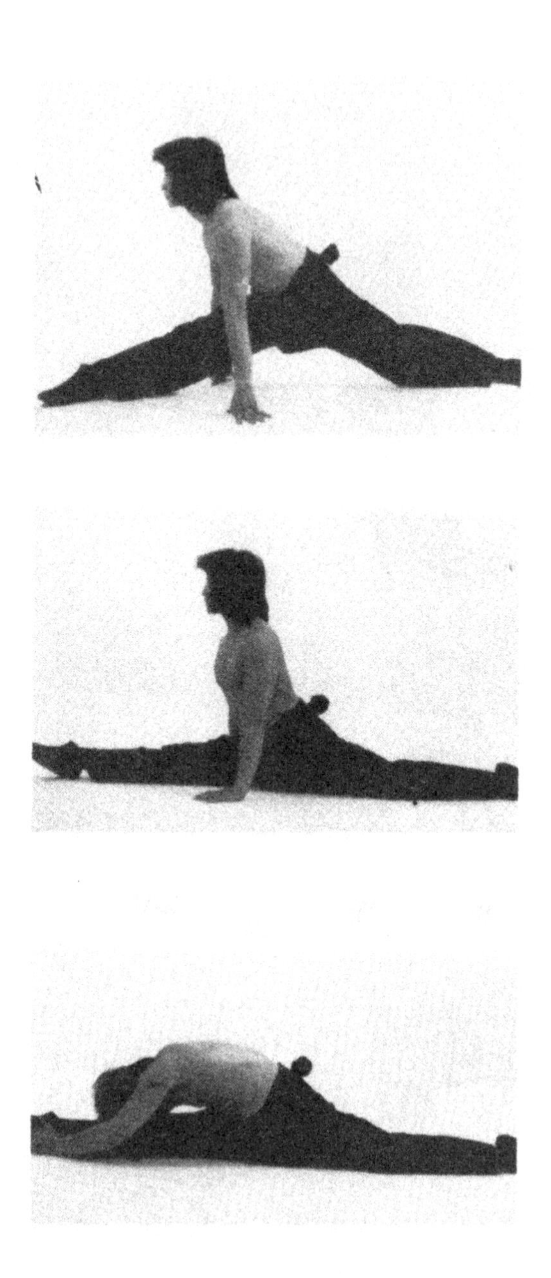

**Splits**

Separate your legs by extending your feet to your front and rear until both are completely extended and flat on the floor.

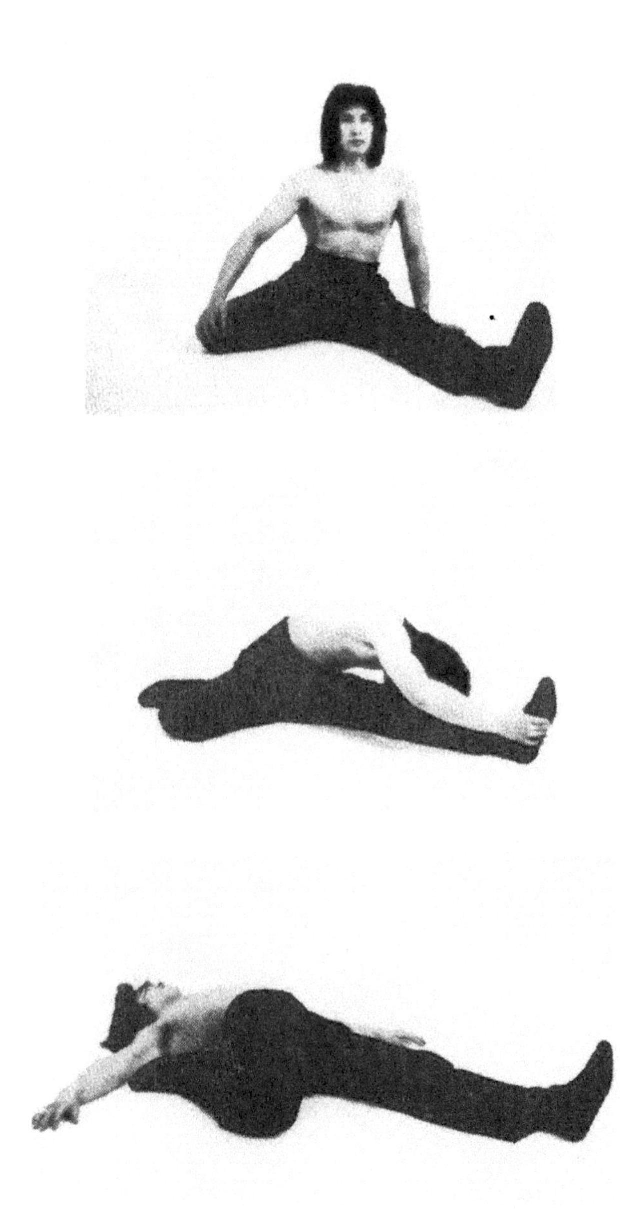

**Single-Leg Sitting-Stretch**

Sit on the floor with your left leg extended to your front and your right leg folded in back of you as illustrated. Grab your left leg and pull your body down over your left leg. Arch back as shown, to stretch the muscles of your upper leg region.

## Snake-Stretch

Begin on hands and knees as shown. Stretch to your rear, pushing your chest as close to the floor as you can, keeping your head down. Now stretch forward creeping close to the floor. Arch your back as you shift forward, pulling your head back as shown.

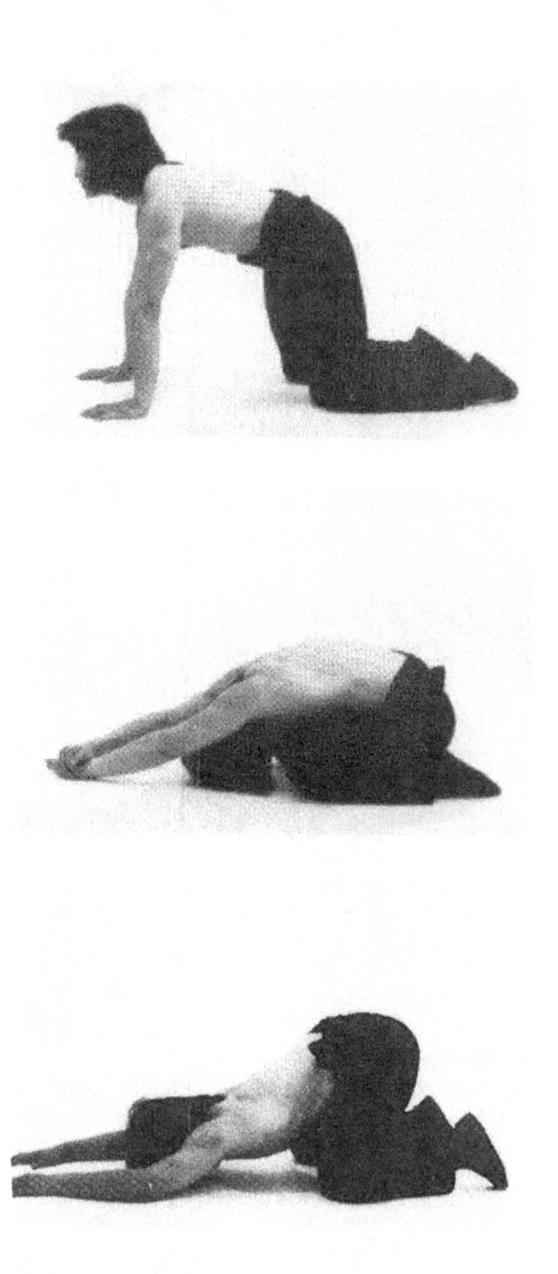

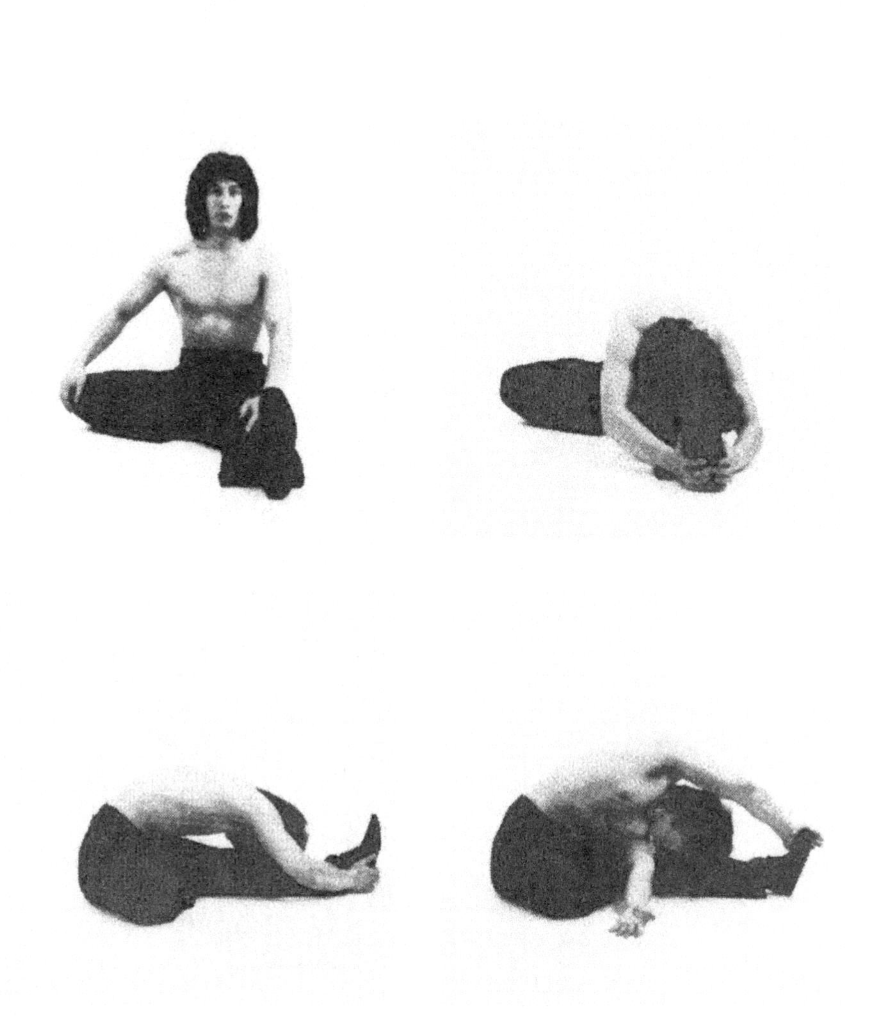

### Single-Leg Sitting-Twist

Sit on the floor with your left leg extended to your front, right leg bent. Your right foot should touch the inside of your left thigh as shown. Grab your left foot and pull your body down to your extended leg. Twist your upper-torso counterclockwise into the position illustrated.

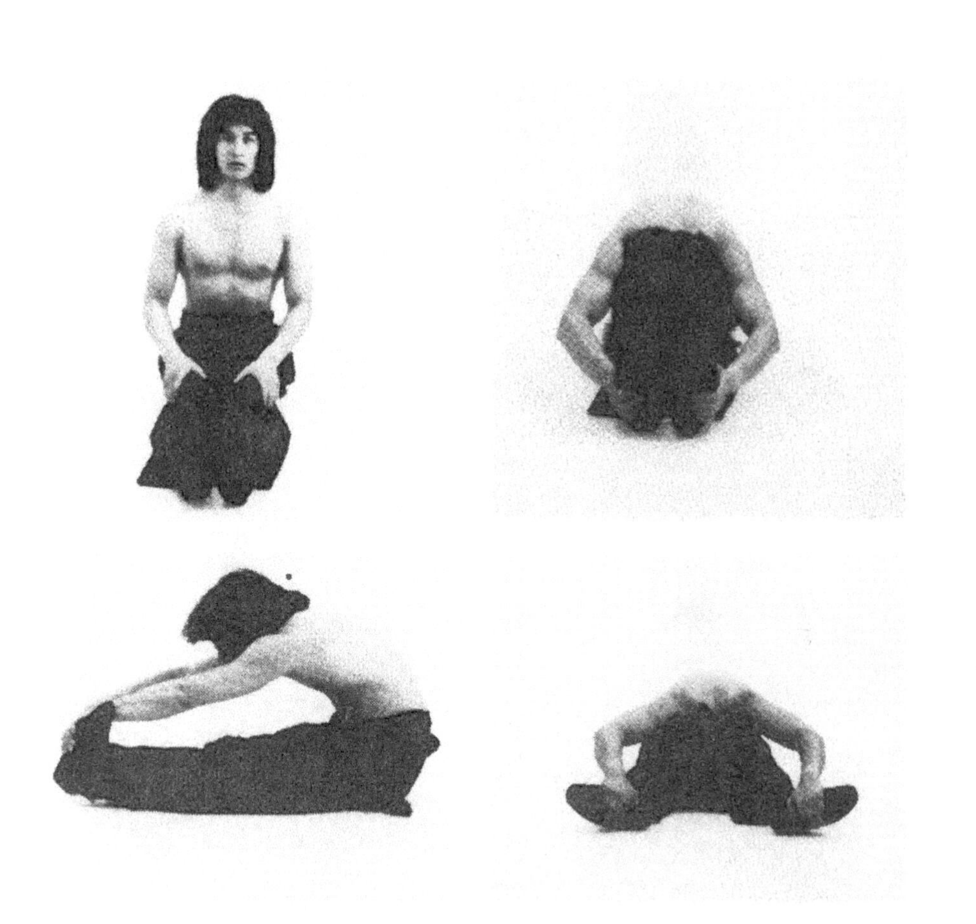

**Sitting, Forward-Stretch**

Sit on the floor with both legs extended to your front. Keep both feet together, your legs straight, and pull your body down to your knees as shown. Separate your legs with your hands and twist your feet from side to side.

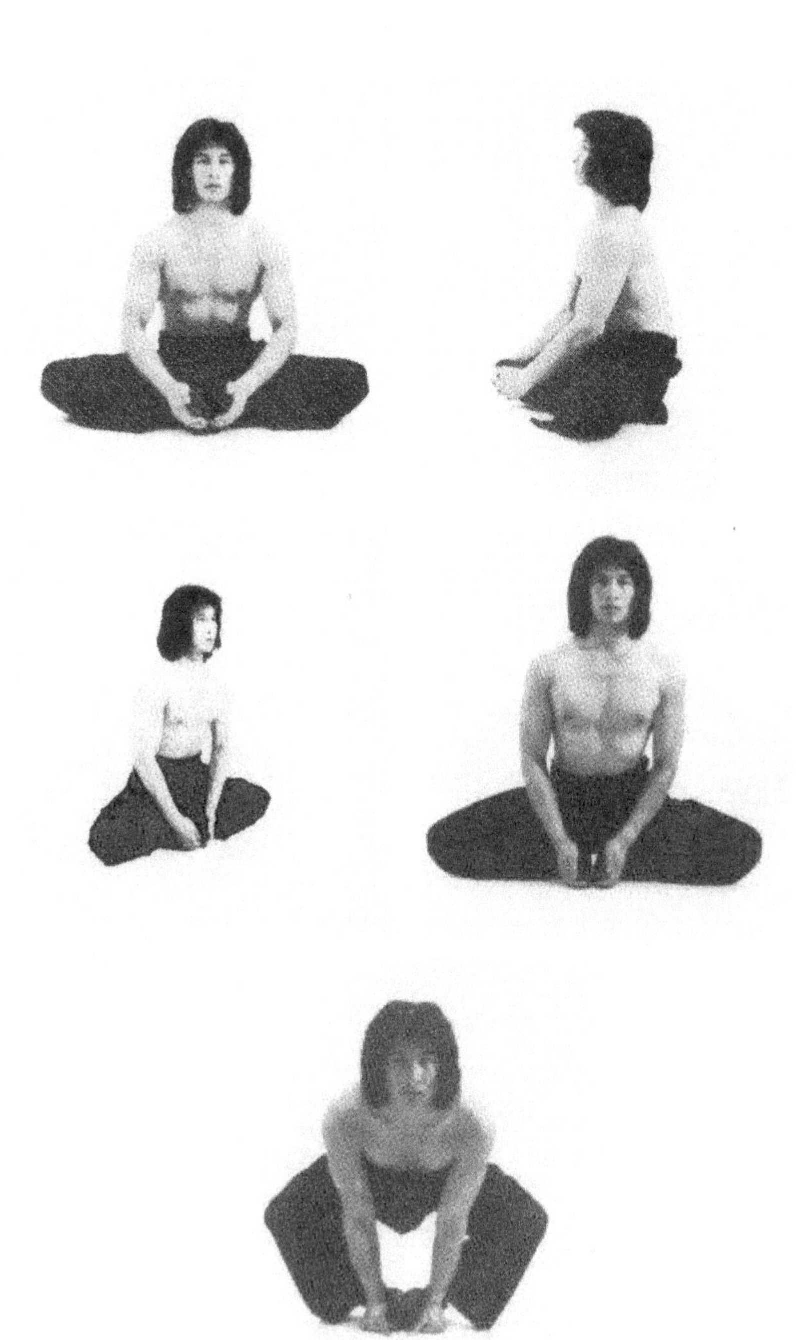

## Butterfly Stretch

Sit on the floor and bring both feet into the position illustrated. Fold your upper-torso forward, placing your weight onto both feet which press together under your body.

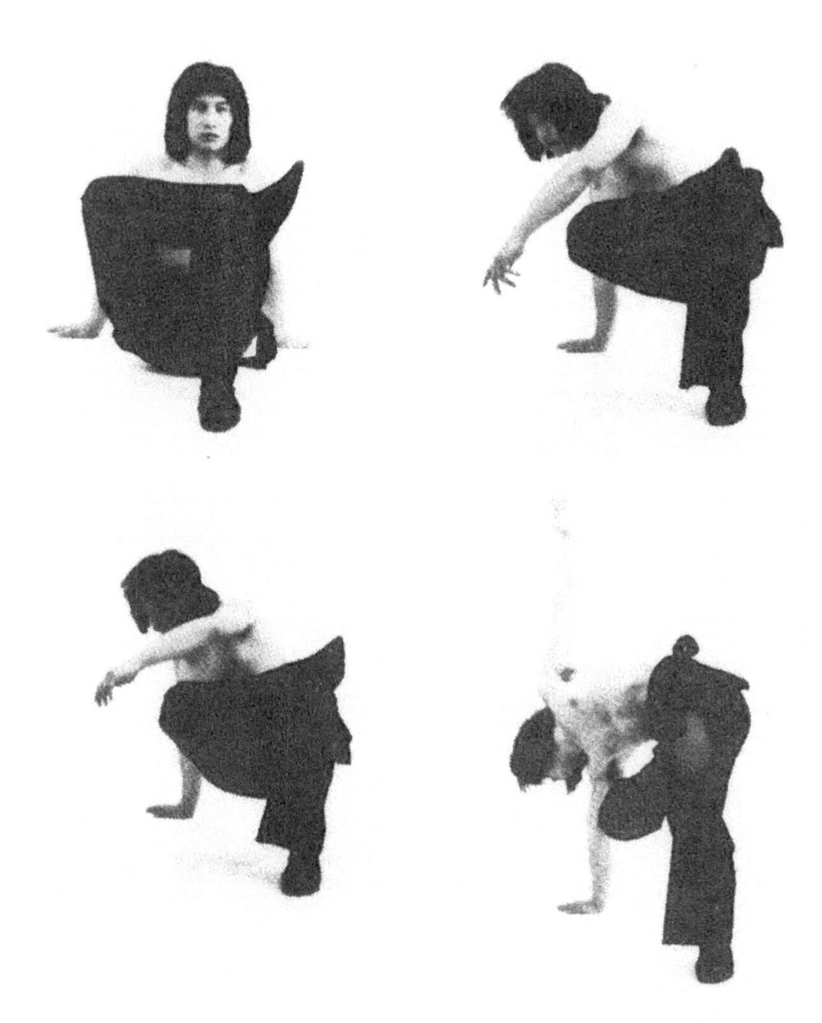

### Cross-Over Stretch

Sit on the floor and place your right leg on top of your left knee as illustrated. Raise up on your left leg and right hand and extend your left hand straight up.

## Circular Leg-Stretch

Sitting on the floor with your legs extended straight out to your front, grab your right foot with your right hand and pull it toward your chest. Maintaining your hold with your right hand, straighten your right leg and wheel it around in a circular motion as illustrated.

### Leg-Lift (Front)

Begin in a normal, relaxed, standing position. Raise your knee as high as you can by grabbing your leg and pulling up. Extend your leg out to your side and hold it as long as you can.

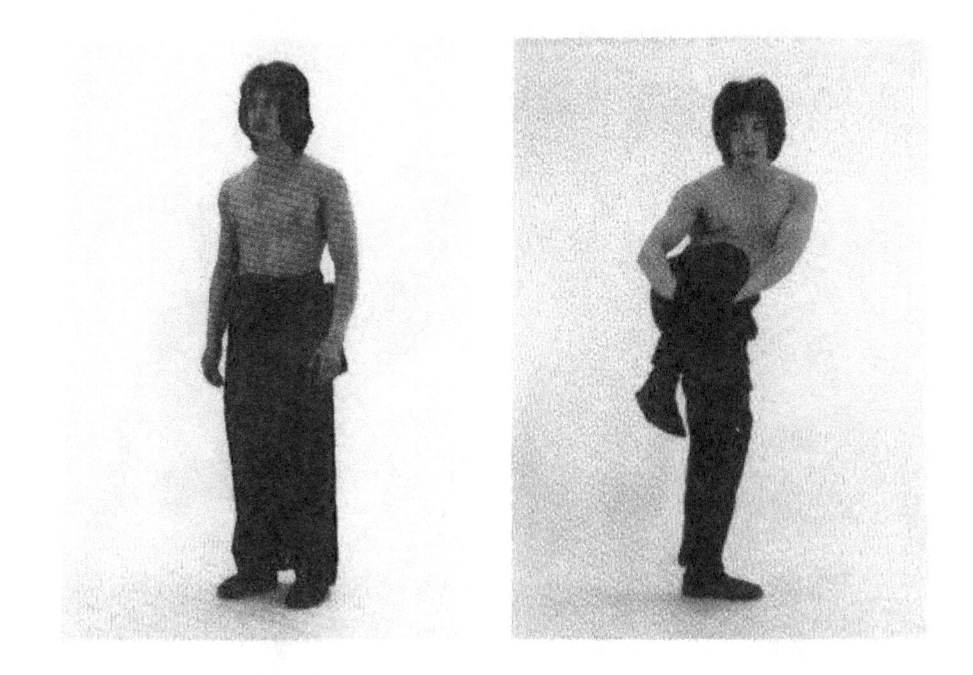

## Leg-Lift (Side)

Twisting to your side, grab your leg with both hands and pull your knee up as shown. Extend your leg out to your side as if kicking and hold it there as long as you can.

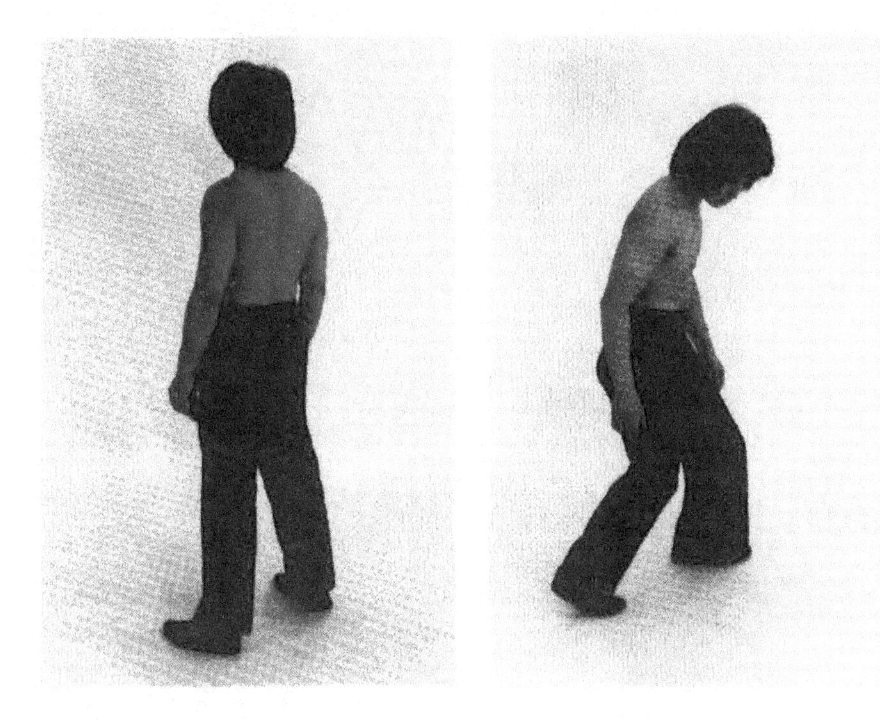

**Twisting-Horse**

Place your feet approximately a shoulders-width apart and, keeping both feet in place, twist counterclockwise, lowering yourself onto your left leg as shown.

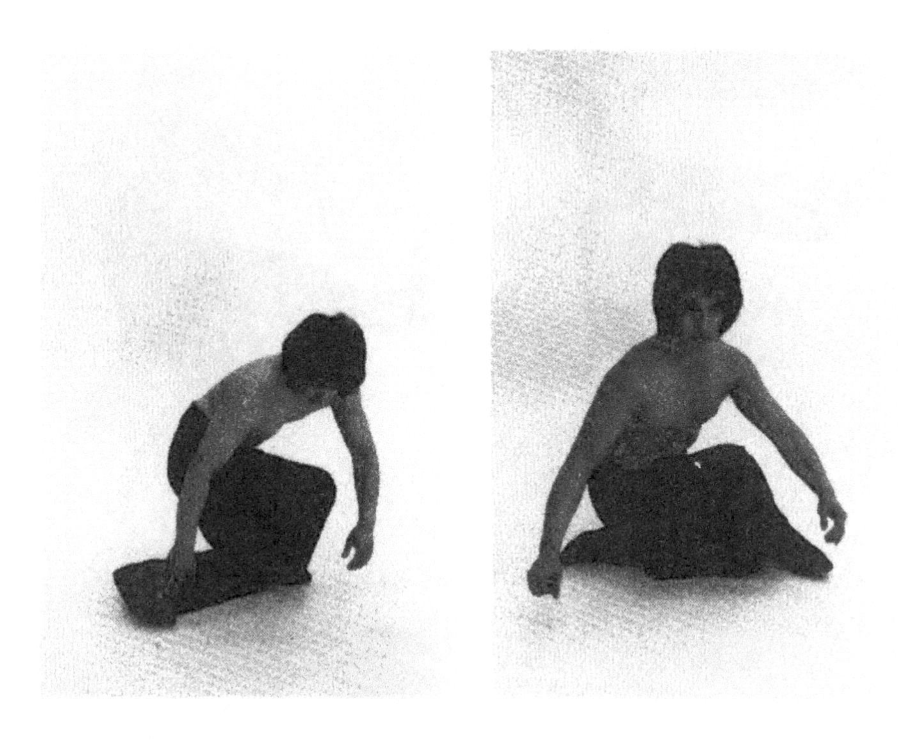

**Single Leg-Bend I**

Begin from a standing position. Extend one leg out to your front and drop down to the floor as illustrated. Without using your hands to aid you, or allowing your extended foot to touch the floor, raise back up to your starting position.

**Single Leg-Bend II**

Begin from a standing position. Folding your foot behind your body, grasp your ankle with your hand and drop down to the floor, touching it lightly with your kneecap. Now return to your starting position by pushing straight up.

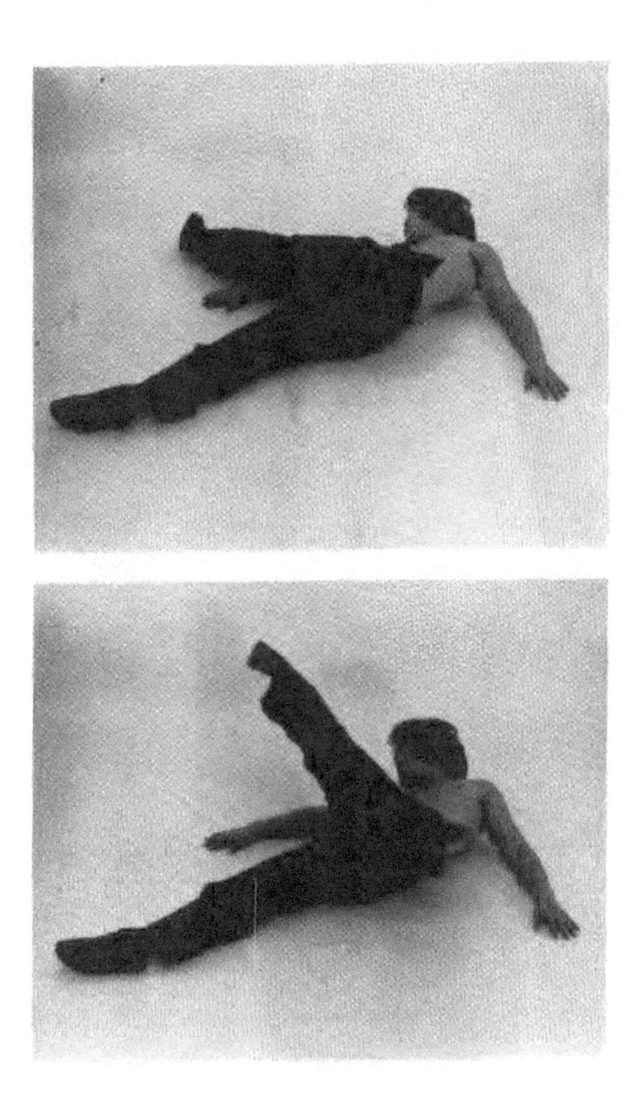

**Leg-Wheels**

Begin by lying flat on the floor as shown. Keeping both legs straight, pivot your hips and bring both legs all the way over to the other side in a smooth arc. Upon completion, reverse the direction (see next page).

Continued on next page.

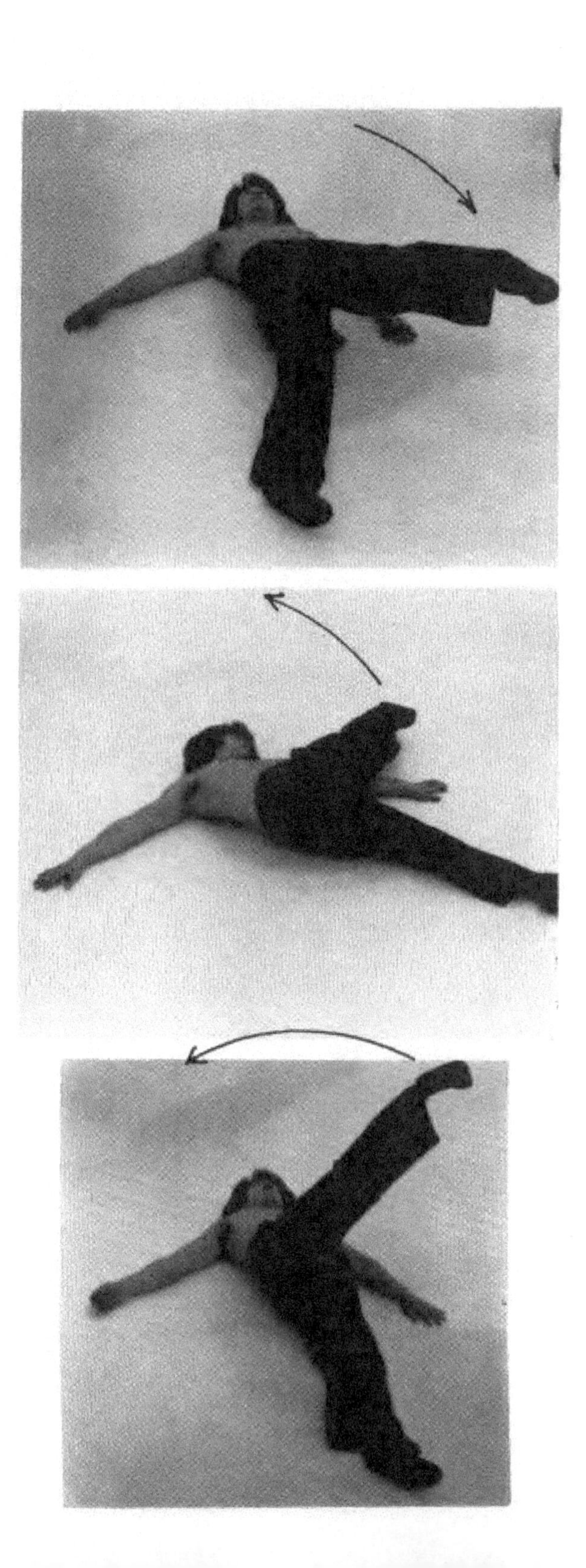

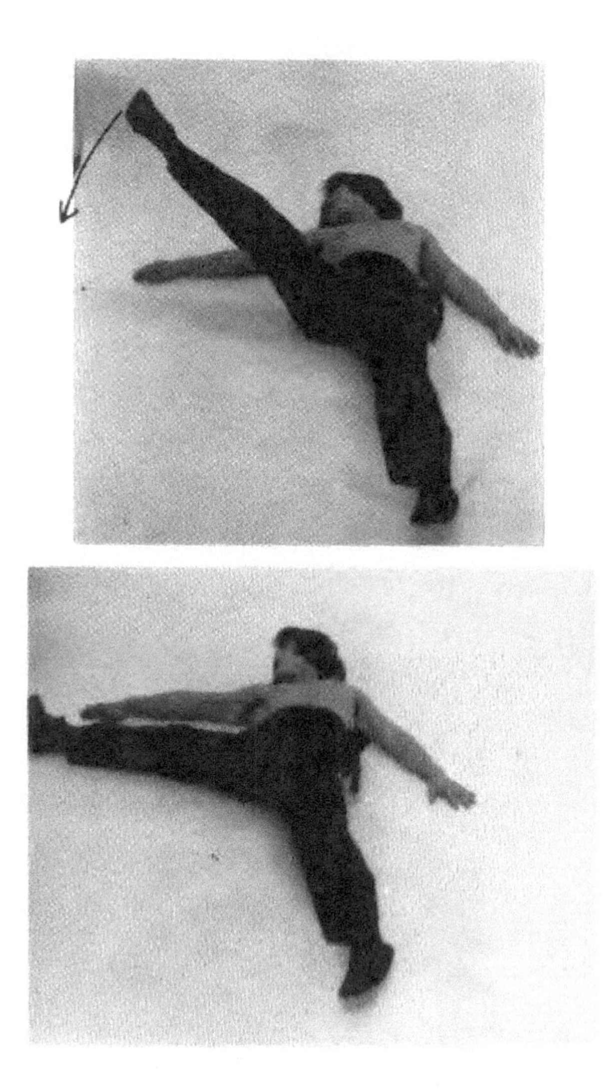

**Bow-and-Arrow Stretch**

Assume a position with your right leg forward, left leg back. Place sixty percent of your weight onto your forward leg which should be bent. Your rear leg is straight. Stretch your upper-torso back, pulling the muscles of your upper leg and hips.

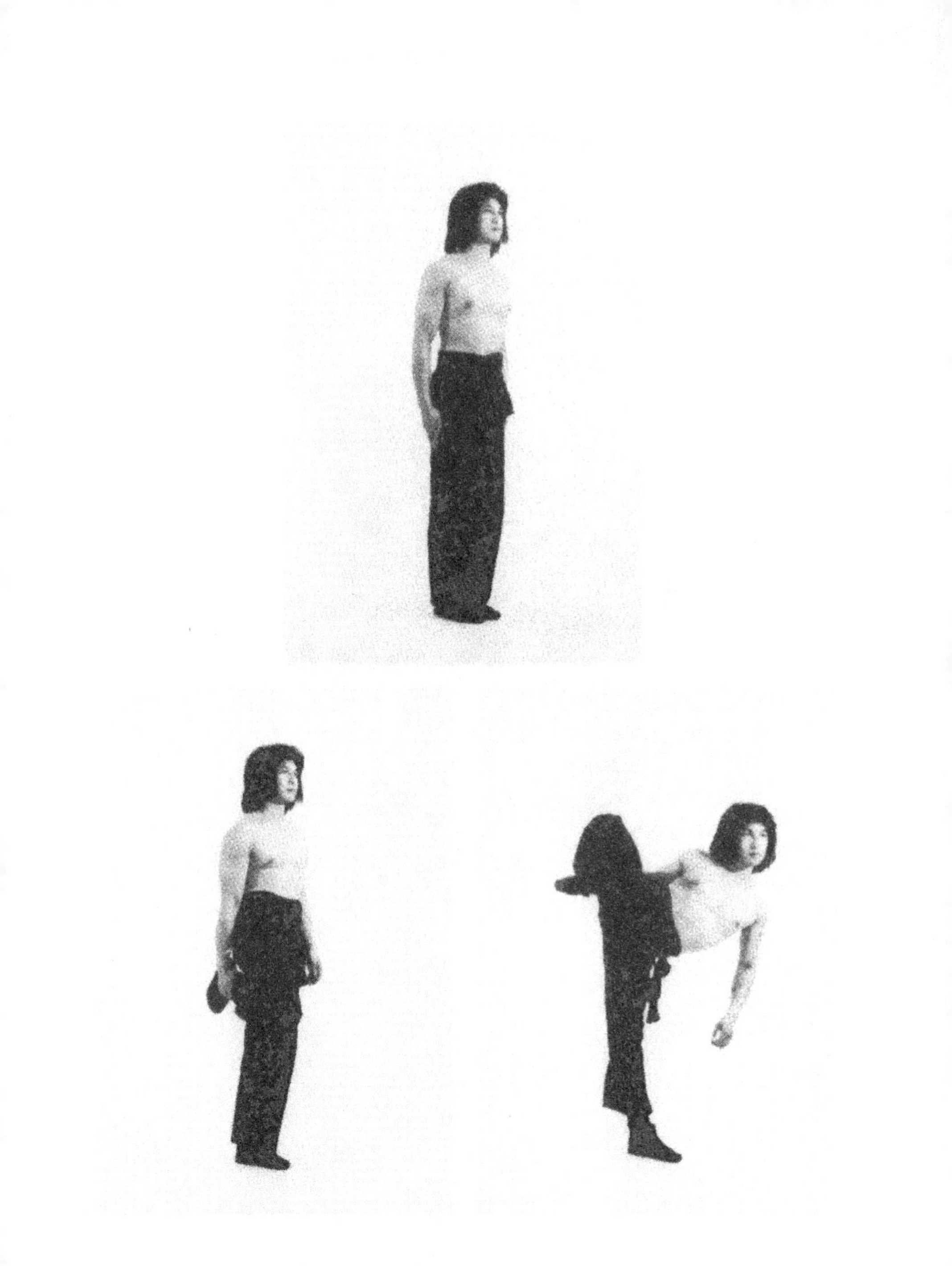

## Knee-Lift

Stand straight up with your feet together and your hands at your sides. Lift your right leg up and grasp your right ankle with your right hand, pulling your leg up as shown. This exercise will help increase your kicking height and balance.

# PART TWO

## Kicking Techniques

Kicking techniques are difficult. There's no getting around it. And in order to master them a student must work diligently. The rewards, however, are great. From a defensive standpoint, the ability to kick well enhances any martial artist's effectiveness as a whole. From a health standpoint, flexibility training is essential to any well-rounded health program.

There are only *so many* ways to kick. You can use one of the striking surfaces illustrated in the previous chapter. Your leg can travel upward or downward, from side to side, forward, or at an angle. And that's about it. But there are an unlimited variety of combinations possible. In this small book, Mr. Lew has taken those kicks which he feels are representative of the movement basic to most northern Kung-Fu kicking techniques. The form of each technique is illustrated first, with a possible method of use following.

Each of the kicks should be practiced on both sides, with either leg, although only one side will be used to demonstrate the maneuver for the text. Needless to say, the student should warm up thoroughly before beginning practice (following the suggested stretching exercises in the front of the book) to guard against pulling muscles or ligaments which may postpone his practice.

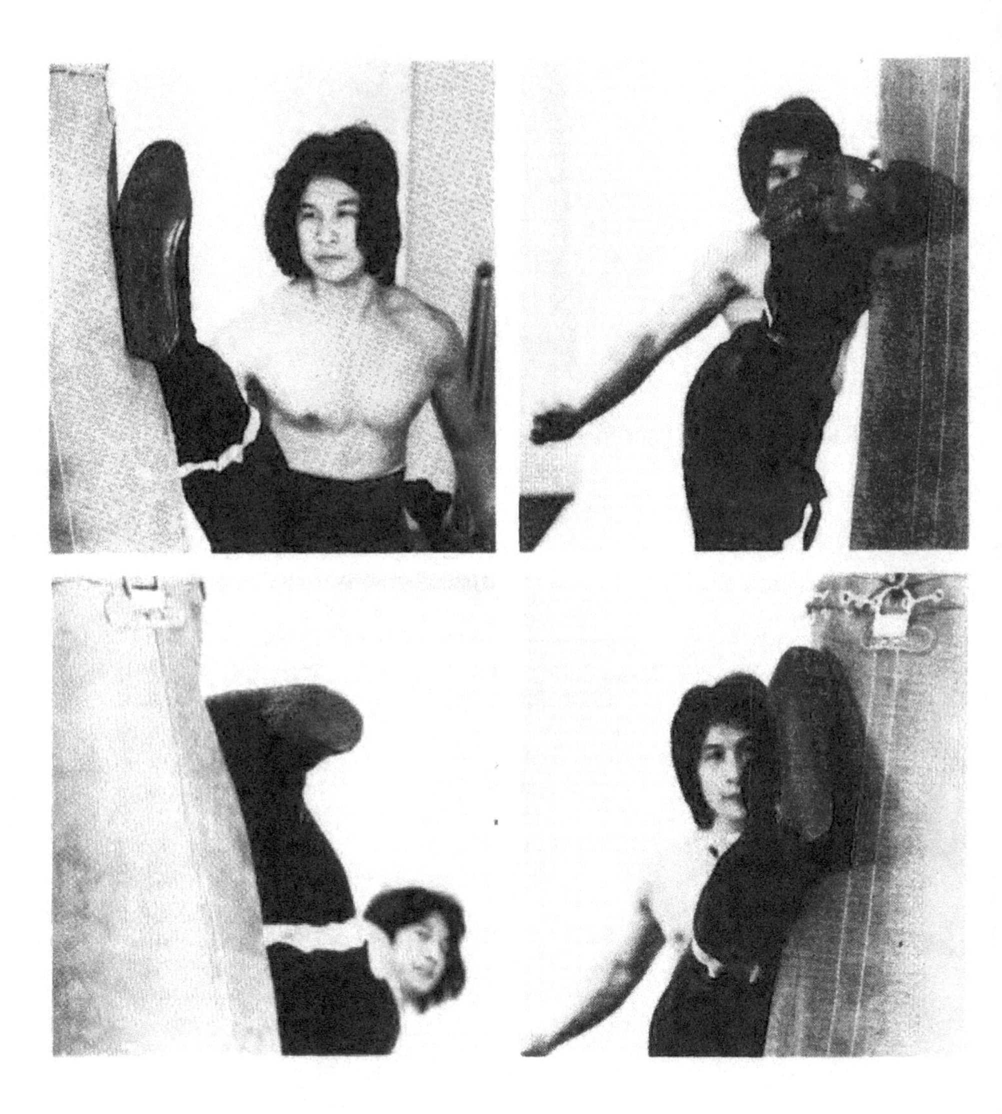

**Striking Surfaces**

Using the proper striking surface of the foot or leg is essential to good kicking. Feet are designed to be walked on, not used as battering rams or bludgeons. In order to both impart the proper force desired and keep from injuring one's ankle, toe, heel or other bones of the foot, a systematic method is used to tighten the ankle.

Do not strike your target with a loose ankle. Always tense your foot to expose the striking surfaces shown here and your chances of escaping injury, even when your kick misses its mark, will be increased tenfold.

## Front Drop Kick

Assume an on-guard position, left foot forward. As your opponent attacks, shift your weight back, dropping down to the floor. Simultaneously shoot your right leg forward, delivering a heel-kick to your target.

**Side Drop Kick**

This is a variation on the front drop kick. In this particular technique, however, fall to the side, cocking your leg as you go down. When your opponent moves into range, shoot a side thrust kick into his solar plexus.

### Foot-Sweep

Assume an on-guard position, left leg forward. Twist your left foot thirty degrees clockwise. Shift your weight onto your left foot, arcing your rightfoot around two hundred degrees clockwise. Keep the sole of your foot in contact with the ground during the entire maneuver.

## Roundhouse

Assume an on-guard position, right leg forward. Shifting your weight back onto your left leg, quickly draw your right knee up. Pivot on your left foot, jerking your hips around counterclockwise so the heel of your left foot points in the direction of your line of attack. As your hips jerk counterclockwise, shoot your right foot out, delivering your kick with the instep of your right foot.

### Lotus Kick

Assume an on-guard position, right leg forward. Shifting your weight onto your right leg, draw your left foot up next to your right. Lifting your right knee, point the sole of your right foot to your left. Arcing your right foot up and clockwise, deliver a right-sweeping kick to your target with the top of your right foot, jerking your hips clockwise.

### Double Side-Kick

Assume an on-guard position, right foot forward. Shifting your weight back onto your left foot draw your right foot up, then kick out to your right side as shown. Quickly retract your right foot and, using the same motion, kick to your right side again, this time aiming for the higher target. The lower kick can be used as either a fake or as an actual kick.

**Side Heel-Kick**

This particular technique is ideal in a multiple attack situation. Begin, as always, in the on-guard position, left foot forward. Utilizing your peripheral vision, you spot a second attacker moving in from the side and quickly shift your weight onto your left foot, drawing your right knee up as illustrated. Whip your right leg up to your right side, striking with an upward blow. Use the heel of your right foot to strike with.

**Roundhouse Heel-Kick**

Assume an on-guard position, left foot forward. Shifting your weight onto your left leg, draw your right knee up as shown and twist counterclockwise, pivoting on your left foot. Your shoulders face forward. As your hips rotate around counterclockwise, snap your right leg forward striking your target with the heel of your right foot.

### The Hook-Kick

Assume an on-guard position, right foot forward. Shifting your weight onto your right leg, quickly draw your left foot up next to your right. Lift your right knee up while twisting your hips counterclockwise and pivot on your left foot so your right heel points in the direction of your line of attack. Kick up, circling around with your right foot, hooking to your right. The striking surface used here is the heel of your right foot. This kick can be performed with either the forward or the rear leg.

### Lift-Kick with Forward Leg

Assume an on-guard position, right leg forward. Shifting your weight onto your right leg, draw your left foot up next to your right and arc your right leg up. Keep your right leg straight and your right toe pointed.

## Lift-Kick with Rear Leg

Assume an on-guard position, left side forward. Shifting your weight onto your left foot, draw your right leg forward. Keep the toe of your right foot pointed straight ahead and arc your leg directly up in front of you as illustrated.

## Butterfly Kick

Assume an on-guard position, right leg forward. Shifting your weight onto your right leg, jump into the air. Lifting your left knee as high as you can, snap your right foot up, kicking with the top of your right foot.

## Inside Crescent-Kick

Assume an on-guard position, left foot forward. Shifting your weight onto your left foot, wheel your right leg around counterclockwise, arcing up directly to your front. Keep your right leg straight throughout the entire move. Slap the inside of your right foot with the palm of your left hand as your right foot reaches the apogee of its arc.

## Outside Crescent Kick

Assume an on-guard position, right leg forward. Shifting your weight onto your right leg draw your left foot up next to your right foot and arc your right leg around in a clockwise manner. The striking surface used for this kick is the outside portion of your ankle. The direction of the strike, when using your right leg, is from left to right.

## Spinning Jump Crescent Kick

Assume an on-guard position, left leg forward. Shifting your weight onto your left leg, draw your right foot up next to your left. Simultaneously jump into the air and spin three hundred sixty degrees clockwise, whipping your right leg around and up as shown.

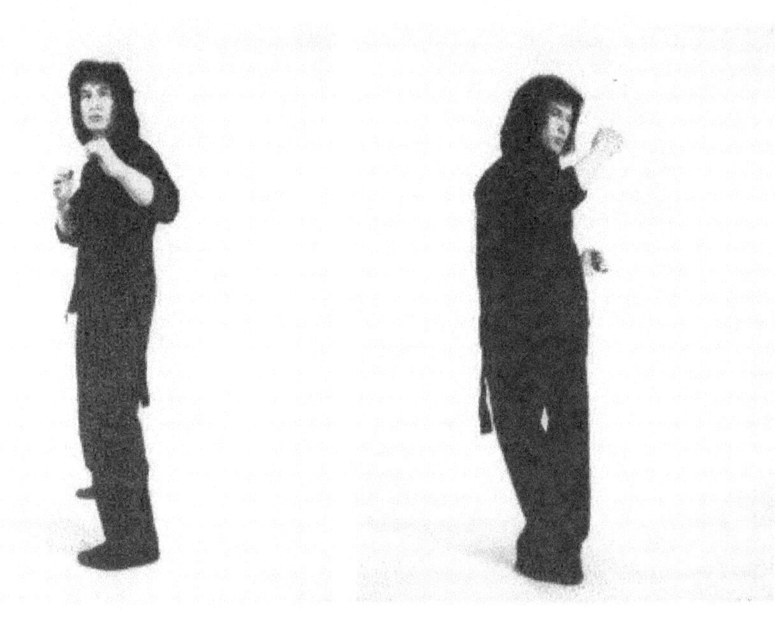

## Spinning Outside-Crescent

Assume an on-guard position, left foot forward. Pivoting on your left foot, twist your entire body one hundred eighty degrees clockwise. Looking over your right shoulder, continue to spin another one hundred eighty degrees clockwise, whipping your right leg around as shown. Keep your right leg straight during its one hundred eighty degree arc.

## Outward Jumping Crescent Kick

Assume an on-guard position, right leg forward. Shift your weight onto your right leg and jump into the air, pulling your left knee as high as you can. Arc your right leg around and up in a clockwise manner as illustrated.

**Inside Spinning, Jump Crescent (From Kneeling Position)**

From the kneeling position shown, jump into the air and twist one hundred eighty degrees counterclockwise spinning off with your right leg. Whip your right leg around to the position shown, striking your target with the inside portion of your right foot. Twist your head quickly around counterclockwise to view your target. The faster you turn your head, the more spin will be imparted to the kick.

## Back-Sweep with Back Spinning-Crescent

Assume an on-guard position, left foot forward. As your opponent attacks, drop down into a sweep position and whip your right leg around clockwise. As your opponent avoids your initial sweep, continue your clockwise turn another one hundred twenty degrees. As your opponent readies himself for his next attack, jump into the air, spinning clockwise and arc your right leg around as shown.

(Continued on next page)

Application of Back-Sweep with Back Spinning Crescent.

### Inside Crescent with Side Kick

Assume an on-guard position, right foot forward. As your opponent kicks for your midsection, shuffle to your right with your right foot and twist counterclockwise, avoiding his attack. Quickly execute an inside crescent kick, arcing your leg up and over his. Shoot your right leg out in a side-thrusting manner, buckling the leg upon which your opponent stands.

(Continued on next page).

Application of Inside Crescent with Side Kick.

## Hinge Kick

Assume an on-guard position, right leg forward. Shifting your weight onto your right leg, draw your left foot up close to your right. Snapping your hips counterclockwise, whip your right leg up. Twist your right knee downward, flipping the outside of your foot into your opponent's face. As your foot drops back to its natural position, snap

your hips clockwise and whip your foot up into your opponent's face from the other side. Your right foot should trace the path of a circle with the opponent's head as the top of the circle and your knee as the center point.

**Grab and Leg Sweep Combination**

Assume the on-guard position, left foot forward. After evading your opponent's punch, grasp his wrist firmly with your right hand and use his momentum to jerk him forward and down, pulling him off balance. Simultaneously, bring the rear leg around smartly in a smooth arc, sweeping his forward leg out from under him.

**Jumping Inside Crescent Kick**

Assume the on-guard position, right foot forward. Neutralize roundhouse with a double softhand block. Pivot on right foot and spin. Halfway around, jump off right leg and kick with the left. This movement will bring you all the way around, putting you in a position to throw inside crescent kick with right leg.

**Back Spinning Heel Kick**

Assume the on-guard position, left foot forward. When the punch is initiated, use a downward block and simultaneously, grab your opponent's wrist. At the same time, pivot on your left foot, spin 360 degrees. Half-way around extend your right leg and plant the heel of your foot in the back of your opponent's head.